The Stifled Poem

The Stifled Poem

An Anthology

Mavis Donner

Bonney Books

CONTENTS

1 | Ode to my Home 1

2 | On a Winter's Day in the Prater 3

3 | Spring in the Stadtpark, Vienna 4

4 | My Garden 5

5 | My Chestnut Tree in Spring 6

6 | The Chestnut Tree at my Balcony 7

7 | Feathered Songsters 8

8 | Spring 2020 9

9 | The Lost Finch 10

10 | The Swan 11

11 | 'Mind the Gaps' 12

CONTENTS

12 | The Chiropodist   13

13 | Chocolate Power   14

14 | Vienna's Coffee Houses   16

15 | Comment on "The Scream"   17

16 | The Hundertwasserhaus   18

17 | Contemplation of van Gogh's
"Haystacks in Provence"   19

18 | The Potato Eaters   20

19 | It Still Writes   21

20 | My Sister's Gods   22

21 | Nightmares   24

22 | My Mother   26

23 | Madame Curie Speaks   27

24 | The Mephisto Waltz   28

25 | The Wrecks of our Lives   29

26 | The Storm: "Dennis the Menace"   30

CONTENTS

27 | Queuing Up   31

28 | A Giant Sequoia in Dolná Krupá   32

29 | Time   33

30 | Total Solar Eclipse 1999   34

31 | The Lesson (a dramatic poem)   36

32 | Train Number 000   38

33 | The Pianist   40

34 | The Philatelist   41

35 | Sorting Socks   43

36 | St Valentine's Day   45

37 | The Office   46

38 | The Alhambra Court of Lions   48

39 | The Skeleton from B.C.   49

40 | Much Ado About Something   51

41 | Murphy's Law   53

CONTENTS

42 | The Dilemma 55

43 | Tipsy Mice 57

44 | The Road to Lakagígar 59

45 | The Icelandic Goðafoss 60

46 | The Blue Lagoon 61

47 | Kjölur Route 63

48 | Icebergs 65

49 | The Bridge of Avignon 66

50 | Traces of You 67

51 | On the Slow Lane 68

52 | Nothing Much 69

53 | Obsession 70

54 | Thinking About Risks 71

55 | The Exemplary Bee 73

56 | The Neighbour's Cat 74

CONTENTS

57 | Mosquito Power 76

58 | The Seagull's Flight 77

59 | Snake Around the Neck 78

60 | The Spider's Web 79

61 | The Answering Machine 80

62 | The Push-Button 81

63 | The Alarm's Rude Awakening 82

64 | City Noises at Night 84

65 | Mirror Images 86

66 | Night Light (motion sensor) 87

67 | Castle Fantasy 89

68 | The Loreley 91

69 | The Museum Artifact 92

70 | The Stifled Poem 94

71 | The Streets of Oxford 95

CONTENTS

72 | The Blue Grotto of Capri   97

73 | Spirit of the Catacombs   99

74 | Through the Channel Tunnel   102

75 | The Ice Cream Man   104

76 | A Mechanical World?   106

77 | Morse Code   108

78 | Stranger   109

79 | The Workaholic   111

80 | The Intercity Express Train   112

81 | Yesterday's Leaves   113

82 | The Telescope   114

83 | The Covid-19 Pandemic   116

84 | The Masked Year   117

85 | The Whistling Poet   119

86 | The Full Stop   120

To my dear son, Ralf

Ode to my Home

You are wherein I spend days and nights
And never thought of singing your praises
But even when we left and took flights
To exotic lands and foreign places
You stood, a waiter, welcoming us back
Or like the faithful spouse eager to please
But I have always taken you for granted
Like my old and dusty front door mat
I just ignored you and hung up the keys
But today you are all that I ever wanted
What has changed so much so quickly?
A disease from which many have died
So we are confined to home indefinitely
And now I see you as a lover his bride
In our living room I can dance and sing
Here I sit and read, here I sit and write
Here I sit and think, here I sit and dream
And when the sun shines, life is bright
And while no ships pass the canal stream
The Danube water shines green and white
How special you are, my spacious home

And how cosy all your rooms and airy
Upstairs and downstairs I get to roam
And peep into books from the library
And there are the big balconies for sun
And the high windows for air and light
Here in this home we are united as one
No sickness here, no plague, no plight
This is a chorale to you, my snuggly place
No 'prison' — for mine is the luxury of space

Mavis Donner, March 2020

On a Winter's Day in the Prater

I walk along the Prater Hauptallee
On a cold and sunny winter's day
There are people everywhere
They are not heading anywhere
There are joggers, there are walkers
There are people with kick scooters
They are very busy with their feet
But in their eyes there's nothing to read
Like the rows and rows of chestnut trees
Shorn of flowers and shorn of leaves
Looking at me with vacant stare
In April they will spring me a flare
The ducks in the lake greet me with glee
They think I've brought a snack with me

Jan. 2020

Spring in the Stadtpark, Vienna

It's April, April again in the park
Is it the red-breasted robin I hear
Or is it the full-throated happy lark
Piping to his mate his songs of cheer?
A warm glow sheds light on steeple and spire
As the sun long lost behind a black sky
Rides once again in her chariot of fire
Daffodils curtsy in the wind, birds fly high
It's that spritely youthful time once more
When Nature is dressed in brightest green
When dazzling flowers carpet the garden floor
When old people think and young people dream
'It's spring,' the cherry blossoms say to me
'Time to be free as that bird in my tree'

4

My Garden

It's that time of the year once more
When my garden in her flimsy finery
Adorned with glittering jewellery
Exudes the perfumes of a whore
Butterflies flit past her door
Birds sing their love-sick ditty
Bees slip in to suckle her honey
Drunk on her wine, they feast at her store
From my window I study her flushed face
The splendour of her changing dress
While I listen to the birds' lust
Every year again I count the days
Every year again I watch her stress
As slowly she withers into dust

My Chestnut Tree in Spring

Spring has come and my dazzling chestnut tree
Is queening herself in her flowery dress
Feeling as happy as happy can be
Proud and tall she stands, eager to impress
Nestling birds warbling the lifelong day
Cradling their young ones in her arms
Would that it were always April and May
When Nature herself is drawn to her charms
But when her pretty dress turns to green
And with the wear and tear of time — to brown
My chestnut tree will be shorn of her sheen
She shivers to think of that dressing down
But today is the Now, today the fun
For tomorrow old November will come

23 April, 2015

The Chestnut Tree at my Balcony

Autumn has come and she looks a sorry plight
Shorn off her nice spring dress all leafy-green
The dazzling gown that crowned her beauty queen
Now her shoulders sag, her body is lean
She awaits the snow to dress her in white
When she'll stand again proud in the night
For those who pass — to stop, to stare, to dream
While she looks them down in her powdery sheen
She knows when it's dark she alone will beam
So head erect she sighs for that frosty light

Christmas 2014

Feathered Songsters

I look for you in wood and dale
Alas how bare the fields, how still the hills
Oh to hear the sounds of starlings' trills
Or the lyric of a nightingale
Away with snow, away with sleet
Oh to see a thrush upon a tree
To hear a songster trill so sweet
How lovely that would truly be
Pipers far away in sunny lands
Filling forests with happy song
The Vienna Woods await your coming home
Now pigeons roost around in gangs
They coo and coo the whole day long
Your lesser cousins, they never roam

Spring 2020

I hear a spritely step outside my flat
And someone rap-rapping at my door
It's happy Spring with her yellow hat
She looks at me, smiles, and says hello
'Why are you not out?' she asks with a smile
'I'm back again, just step outside and look
Daffodils, whose beauty will only last a while
Crocuses and tulips beside the rippling brook
I've touched the buds, they've brushed off sleep
Out your window the yellow forsythias call 'Hi'
But you keep away from the flowers and heat
Why don't you step outside... or tell me why'
'Dear Spring, a virus has us in its deadly grip
We shut the door in its face, to give it the slip'

March 2020

The Lost Finch

At breakfast I saw a bird on my balcony
A small red-headed finch singing a song
His lyric was so sweet, so melancholy
I could listen on and on all day long
I thought how nice of him to sing to me
What a compliment from so small a thing
'Is that your nest up my chestnut tree?'
I asked, all eager to open talk with him
'Come in,' I invited as I went to the door
To let my guest in from the blustery rain
'I've bread and water for you on the floor
Why's your song so sad — like a cry of pain?'
Just then I heard a long and lonesome call
He cocked his head and was gone from the wall

Feb. 2020

The Swan

The sun is setting on the Danube river
Red, blue, gold suffusing the darkening sky
It's cold and chilly and I feel a shiver
As I watch the ships go by, light and spry
Swish swoosh, swish swoosh over the water
Waltzing in rhythm to their destination
It would be nice were it slightly warmer
To the full to enjoy Nature's creation
Should I up and go or should I simply stay?
The answer glides past in royal dress
A bird as white as snow comes my way
He pirouettes. This is Swan Lake I guess
I look at him and he looks at me
We are as happy a pair as can be

Jan. 2020

'Mind the Gaps'

You wait, your heart beating, it's hard to swallow
And while others sit still, you can hardly breathe
You fidget, moisten your lips, wish for tomorrow
You're angry, regretful, how you hate your teeth
Your name rings out, you want to escape, to run
In his chair, anaesthesia numbs your feeling
The dentist's syringe pokes into your gum
You feel dazed, your head is turning and reeling
The nurse suctions the saliva from your throat
Like Prometheus Bound your nerves are tightly wound
A cave digger, he probes and pokes, and you choke
As he drills, your head, a top, is spinning round
'I've cleaned and stopped the gaps,' you hear him say
Just as you're out the door, waltzing on your way

The Chiropodist

In her expert hands, my lustreless feet
Are soon restored to health and heat
This is a woman concerned with both
She pulls at the toes and rubs each sole
With cream of chamomile and vitamin E
In her hands I am as relaxed as can be
She studies my fully exposed toes
Like a soldier attacking her foes
The ghastly ingrown nail she winches
With one tug from her cuticle nippers
The corn she chisels and scrubs
And dabs with disinfectant rubs
Her eyes study my feet like a laser
Deftly using a file and a shaper
I look at my lovely feet in shock
They are rearing to go for a walk

Chocolate Power

Have you wondered how an ant must feel
when it stumbles onto a sugar hill —
whether it is enthralled by the dizzy heights,
whether it dreams that sweet days will never end,
whether it sickens from overconsumption.
Abundance has soft ways of killing.
I work in a chocolate factory
from early morning till late afternoon.
I stand clad in white overalls and gloves
inspecting the choc-a-bloc bars
riding on the conveyor belt.
I have the eyes of a microscope:
nothing can escape my scrutiny.
I see a tiny blob, a smear, a scar
on a fragment of a chocolate bar.
Anything not completely flawless
goes straight to the recycling bin.
I sometimes see the stream
of factory visitors filing in,
glutting their eyes on the liquid chocolate,
rows upon rows and rows of gooey slabs.

With what ecstasy they contemplate
the huge mounds of mass production.
How they luxuriate in the smell
of vanilla and cocoa powder.
And I reckon they must wish to be me —
behind the walls of a chocolate house,
a fairy-tale Gretel without the witch.
But the truth is, I have quite a surfeit.
The smell of sugar and chocolate butter,
the overpowering smell of pile upon pile
of chocolates, thousand times multiplied
hanging in the air, creeping round corners,
suffocates me with its sickening sweetness.
It penetrates my everywhere:
my nostrils, my ears, my hair.
It seeps into the pores of my skin.
It follows me home and even to bed,
folding itself surreptitiously
around the sheets and pillow cases.
The smell of chocolate invades my dreams.
Abundance has soft ways of killing.

Vienna's Coffee Houses

The trees along the Danube shake in fear
The leaves, they tremble — gone their russet glow
They hear the howling storm approaching near
They know this Arctic beast will blow and blow
To coffee houses people wend their way
They step into a world of Hapsburg charm
A sphere where Time is captive, Night is day
A sphere where coffee stirs but does no harm
Café Central entices young and old
They chat, they drink their coffees black or white
Consuming Time in sips, they block out cold.
The man who reads his book is bathed in light
I scan the title: 'Nineteen Eighty-Four'
Did Orwell sit there once beside the door?

Comment on "The Scream"

A sick sun suffused all in ghostly light
Trees shivered, leaves quivered in orange glow
I heard it then that awful cry of fright
Its shrill vibrations echoing high and low
There 'It' stood — he, she it, I could not tell —
Black hole for mouth, wide saucers for eyes
Both hands raised to ears — to quell its yell?
The woods shuddered, beasts ran for their lives
Was it not the cry of primeval man
Driven from Eden for breaking a ban?

Christmas 2018

The Hundertwasserhaus

Jolted from straight thinking, I gape
The house, crooked, an odd sight
Hues — yellow, blue, white, catch the summer light
Slanted in every which way in curvy shape
I think of Antoni Gaudí, of butterflies' wings
I think of prisms, rainbows, of coloured balls
The village is all wavy with shops and stalls
While the façade glitters, a robe for queens
A stairway ripples its way to a balcony
Like a rainbow wave in the distant ocean
The flats are green with a hanging garden
But my eyes get used to this crooked harmony
I think of Thoreau and his spell with Nature
But if the truth be told it fits no mould
It has no before or after, it is bright and bold
A monument to the best in art and sculpture

17

Contemplation of van Gogh's "Haystacks in Provence"

Autumn's work is done, I'm finished for the day
Every blade of grass, yellow, green or brown
Falls upon my scythe, mown down where it lay
My ladder shoves me up the hayrick crown
My neck strains, my arms ache to thatch the stack
But still it's skill that spawns a work of art
I make hay while the sun shines on my back
Gathering the grass without a cart
But fodder for winter is now all there
Come hail, come snow, my cows will eat
It's time to dance and sing, without a care
The waning sun will still give us heat
So year by year the reaper mows his fields
For when winter comes, autumn yields

The Potato Eaters

Round a dimly-lit table, peasants are sitting,
their rough calloused hands and coarse faces
showing traces of soil erosion; no dreaming
idealists dressed in fancy brocade or laces,
just hard-living peasants, potato eaters,
providing for the eyes of onlookers
indelible impressions of earthiness.
Naked nature dressed in brown dyes.
A picture expressing dire scantiness,
Van Gogh ravishes the famished eyes.
His genius lives on and on: it never dies.

It Still Writes

It still writes after all these years
in an unopened handbag
smelling faintly of violets
real or only imagined.
You said it will keep contact —
That was not meant to be.
A faint smell of violets —
is the flimsy unreality
that now still connects.

My Sister's Gods

My sister's room was a god cocoon
Where gods were born and reborn
First she invoked the Buddha — om, om, om
The cry crept through windows and doors
And echoed along the long corridors
To the rooms of the rest of her family
To them she was just crazy or funny
The Buddha gave place to Lakshmi
The Hindu goddess of prosperity
The temple of my sister's room smoked
With wraiths of incense that choked
The goddess was strewn with jasmine
Petals gathered on a daily routine
Now a scented goddess was born
This flowery period came to a quick end
When my sister started going to church
At that time she was doing research
On the Bible which she read till she dozed
She fasted, said her beads, aided the poor
Her gods were lying face-down on the floor.
'Praise the Lord,' they said, 'your sister is reborn.'

Then I got a letter from my sister:
She wrote that her house is open
To all the gods, unknown and known
'I'll not make unfair distinction
Between any god, this my conviction
What if I'm wrong and another right?
What if a new god comes to light?
So my door is ajar to all and sundry
It's okay — all stem from the same tree.'

Nightmares

During the day, the trapdoor leading
to the recessed room in my mind
snaps shut with a silent bang.
But at night, the door is opened wide,
and one by one, the spectres march out
in grotesque forms, washed by the night tide
as incarcerated images incarnated.
The harmless spider I saw on the wall
is that venomous female black widow,
mate eater, and she's sleeping in my bed.
The quiet millipede in my garden,
nestling between the stinging nettle
is now a slithering rattlesnake
between the folds of the dark curtain.
The unopened letter on my desk
flashes danger signals before my eyes.
Out of that blocked toilet needing repair
pops a large grey mouse covered in hair.
That solid suspension bridge by daylight
transforms into a movable monster
swinging me into the rushing water.

I'm sitting coiled up in a knotted ball,
cold-sweating and hyperventilating,
when the air in the cabin depressurises,
and the mechanical bird is in free-fall.
But after night dawns the morning,
when the tired phantoms go to sleep

My Mother

In the garden of her loving heart
Where Nature planted fragrant flowers
Thieving Death has taken nothing more
Than dying petals at the entrance door
From that inner casket still untampered
An immortal perfume spreads unhampered

Madame Curie Speaks

As night by night, I lay awake in bed,
radium aglow within my mind,
the need to find its pure metallic state
became my one obsessive aim in life.
I felt the metal grab and jab my brain,
I felt it bang and break its prison door,
and like a cosmic star, it sent forth rays.
I thought of radium upon the field
of medicine, I thought what potency
radiology my labours' legacy
to man would bring. To give longevity
to mortal man became my haunting aim.
What ecstasy was truly mine when dream
became a living thing, but such a price
I paid, as lethal radiation burnt
my hands and sapped and wasted all my bones.
A stupor crept upon my battered brain,
A languor stole upon my weakened frame.
And now I knock upon your future door.
Radium, a two-edged sword has strength to heal or kill,
so guard it well — with caution and with skill

The Mephisto Waltz

On Las Ramblas in Barcelona
Kermit, the frog, all in bright green
is playing on a small concert grand
Liszt's Mephisto Waltz rumbles through hell,
The virtuoso bowing and grinning,
his webbed feet tapping the earth,
his fingers flying over the keyboard,
his eyes two beads reading the score.
And finishing with a flourish of fingers,
he bows to the clapping of hands.
Behind him under a red lamp,
a lean man wearing black
has been pulling the strings,
his face hidden in the shadows.

The Wrecks of our Lives

Thrown up by waves on to our clean beaches
A bit of this and that, the rags of riches
Plastic bottles, bags and tags, all our waste
Cigarette butts and stuff, all dumped in haste
The sea is a pit for odds and ends and tips
It's a deep bottomless hole, an ancient crypt
Where once we walked and picked up shells
And sat to inhale the fresh and salty smells
Where once we combed the rocks for fossils
And hoped to find messages in bottles
Today we walk the beach and pick up muck
And alas, it all too often smells like yuck
But still I think I hear the sea say
'Save me, save me, for another day'

Feb. 2020

The Storm: "Dennis the Menace"

The wind moaned and groaned in rage
He rattled the windows, banged the doors
I saw, I heard him from my secure 'cage'
His voice jiggled the shutters, shook the floors
It sent shock waves through the silent night
He ground and gnashed his teeth in fury
Eyes flashing fire, showing off his might
He was out to wreak havoc — the big bully
For a whole hour he huffed and he puffed
In vain; he could not bring my house down
I smiled to know that he was not chuffed
His fury spent, he slammed out of town
Nothing but tears remained as I heard the rain
Pitter-patter, pitter-patter on my window pane

25th January, 2020

Queuing Up

I much dislike standing in a queue
And here I am in one a mile long
At the tail end with no clear view
What do I do? Cheer up and sing a song?
Or should I fall asleep counting sheep?
Or forget the fair and go elsewhere?
I watch a man jumping queue, the creep
Like a fox sneaking in from nowhere
Queues I guess exist for such as these
The sly, the brazen, the aggressive type
At Heaven's Gate they'll grab the keys
Will Peter send them to the other side?
But still I think queuing up is good
It makes us into a brotherhood

A Giant Sequoia in Dolná Krupá

You giant sequoia tree from across the sea
Warden of Beethoven's garden, tall and fine
He and you a potent symbol of Timeless Time
Oh how I wish I were as strong and as free
Oh how I wish I were a giant sequoia tree
I marvel at your full crop of green hair
That neither age nor sickness can bare
Oh how I wish I were a giant sequoia tree
With head in the air and feet on the ground
You can see, smell and hear every sound
Beethoven wrote his lilting moonlight song
Some time before you were even sown
Were you there you would have been his Zeus
Were you there you would have been his Muse

Time

Some say the universe is expanding
Some say the universe is contracting
What difference does it make to me?
I, infinitesimal, stand here among others
My right foot forward, my left foot backward
My right arm forward, my left arm backward
Here am I caught in a moment of history
Fossilized along the Great Highway
In the superglue of Time

Total Solar Eclipse 1999

Those who lived along the line of totality
Hoped they'd view the eclipse in entirety
In the weather they put their faith
I considered that extremely brave
People were spanning the bridge
They were everywhere in every niche
While some hiked up craggy hills
Others scaled the castle wall for thrills
They thought it would be so much more fun
To be just that bit closer to the sun
All heads were turned up towards the sky
They hoped that it would stay dry
Eyes peered through black polymer viewers
Among the crowds many sun worshippers
As the moon crept between earth and sun
People laughed, shouted and clapped as one
But that Bright Star seemed to doze off fitfully —
Like one slightly hesitant to let go completely —
It surely was aware that born with a Big Bang
With a whimper to simulate death was not its plan
Excitement abated as rain clouds collected

Those who had converged from all corners
To view this miracle of solar prominences
And fully to glut their eyes on the corona
Groaned, gloom swathing their countenances
Rain pelted, that spoilsport, envious of the sun
A few turned on their heels and started to run
But people clung on hoping for it to stop
But it went on and on falling drop by drop
And then there came the total eclipse play
Changing day to night, keeping day at bay
Like a hand playing with a light switch
Without a hitch, without a glitch
Slowly daylight was switched off
Slowly day into night was morphed
The cheering crowd went delirious
This drama was ever so mysterious
Alas, soon it came to a dramatic end.
Elsewhere, people saw — or thought they had seen
Through the broken cloud, such a fantastic scene:
'A chain of pearls emitting light'
'A night sky studded with stars'
'Brilliant diamonds shining bright'
'A fiery ball as red as Mars'
Such mysteries lurk on the retina of the eye
Such fantastic images our brain lets fly
Under strain or stress we can go awry

The Lesson (a dramatic poem)

Today we'll study sentence problems —
the run-on, the fragment, the comma splice;
grammar, you know, can be rather nice.
Yes, David. Could you repeat that?
Good point. Very good point, in fact.
Yes, some writers tend to ignore grammar.
Where did you see the comma splice used?
Contemporary literature? But of course.
You want to know why some writers use them?
Let me put that to the class.
Right again. You're a bright lot.
Ignorance of the rules or writer's license.
You have your hand up, John.
You say emphasis on ideas rather than style.
Perhaps. I hadn't thought of that.
Sonia, you hold that writers should uphold grammar
and that poetic license means anything goes.
(If I don't get back on track, my distinction is in the bin. I'm
deviating from the lesson plan. That boy again. What does he
want now? Interrupting and disrupting, preying on my already
jangled nerves.)

Yes, David. You want to look into your assigned novel for as
many comma splices as you can gather?
The class and I are with you.
That's a very creative proposal,
since you've got your texts at your disposal.
Go to it. Look for errors in sentence structures
and write down as many as you encounter.

Train Number 000

We sit there locked together in grief:
mothers with children, mothers without,
children bewildered and lonesome,
the surprised men who dodged capture.
We sit there in the boxed train car
like tossed up flotsam on a stormy sea,
our bodies touching, shivering, inhaling
the concentrated grief of our race.
'Where is this train taking us, mother?'
cries the little girl in the little space
with her face all screwed up and tight.
The mother's knobbly hand trembles;
she's sleeping in an abyss of forgetfulness.
'Where's this train taking us, mother?'
Her dazed eyes look at her daughter:
'If only he had not let go of my hand.'
She turns her distracted face to mine,
the stray hair over her eyes clotted with tears:
'If only he had not let go of my hand.
I sat there tense with the feel of fear.
I saw my house sizzling, the fiery

tongues leaping, and the shrieking
cries of my sons; where are those boys now?
I move on — the smouldering remains of me.'
The man with the downcast eyes opens his sack
and displays some water he has saved.
The people crane towards this fountain
like thirsty animals lapping stagnant rain.
When we needed drink, they gave us gall,
When we needed food, they stole our bread.
This exiled unwanted mass of humanity —
'Where is this train taking us, mother?'
'I have no answers, only questions,
only riddles, and the burning Why?
I must blot out the thoughts that materialise.'
'Where is this train taking us, mother?'
'If only... if only I know that they are safe.'
As darkness covers the face of outside,
sleep, like a creeping anaesthesia
takes over, and we sleep that we may die.

The Pianist

(For Ralf)

You sit there, so poised at the grand piano
with your serene and contemplative face,
while I sit coiled, my heart running a race,
watching your fingers, the shape of your hand.
How easily the octaves soar and land
as you fly with 'The Lark' over a maze
of symbolic sound — flats and sharps ablaze.
Tell me something: when did your hands expand
that they run eighty-eight keys of a piano grand?
When did your feet first reach the pedal
and your fingers move from treble to treble?
When were they flying over the whole piano
With that inexplicable skill of a virtuoso?
So the quiet crocus surprises the spring
So the early bird rises and starts to sing

The Philatelist

He is sitting at the table again
with his magnifying glass and tweezers,
examining his vast stamp collection
with the caution of a careful surgeon
performing a delicate operation.
He knows each of his stamps individually:
the damaged serrations on the one,
the flawless countenance of another.
He looks at the watermark and the colours;
he looks for missing stamps in a series,
wishing he could fill the expensive gaps;
he thinks about ones with personal stories.
Watching his obsessive passion,
you'd think a stamp is something else —
not that little bit of nothing
you stick to an envelope with spit.
You think, what is all the fuss about
a collection of miniature pictures
of commemorative events in history?
All those designs and patterns and symbols
and famous people, who knows when dead —

you look at them with a toss of your head —
what are these useless things worth today?
And because you think of value as money,
you can't understand the philatelist,
who will buy a precious stamp, not to seek
a higher price for it, but just to keep.
If you think, however, about character,
it's nicer to live with a collector
who thinks you're indispensable
than with someone to whom you're expendable.

Sorting Socks

Pairing socks out of the washing machine
Is to me a task supreme
The reds and yellows are easy to match
They are the bright pieces the eye can catch
The blacks and greys are often lost
Like all the others they get tossed
Two by two they go into the wash
Out they emerge lost or squashed
And I stand there feeling the dry static
Sorting socks I find is beyond hectic
Here's one neither black nor grey nor pink
For the life of me I don't know what to think
Sometimes I'm staring at a woollen sock
That's shrunk and looks like a blob
And sometimes there's a big hole in the toe
Which certainly wasn't there before
The worst is when suddenly you find
A pale, sickly looking half-green kind
And you know it was lily-white before
Are there still more surprises in store?
There's a poltergeist in that drum

Who's bent on causing harm
He juggles the sizes and numbers
And he even mixes the colours
I prefer counting grains of sand on the sea-shore
To sorting socks, that's for sure

St Valentine's Day

Dear 'Your V',
Why this anonymity?
This would have been my reply to you:
Even without a real name
Even without an address
It was easy to guess
the person behind that blue rose.
Tom, Dick or Harry would have sent red:
red roses with those three clichéd words
But true blue, that's the colour of you
I gaze into the petals of your eyes
and I find myself reeling — drowning
into paradise.

The Office

X is the busiest office
in the entire metropolis —
All you need is an official something,
but it takes a lot more than an evening.
And now I'm going to stop rhyming,
for sure it has become obvious to you
that in such a hectic place,
one cannot afford the luxury
of rhyme, rhythm or meter.
You arrive at the top storey,
the right place for a high office,
with your papers under your arm.
You enter a room where people
are working behind glass barricades.
You sit; you wait to be noticed.
Workers have 'creased' foreheads
A door in your memory opens,
and you see the creased forehead
of your mother bending over your bed,
of your father when the bank statement
arrived at the end of the month,

of students in the big open hall,
waiting for the examination to start.
If you are to read this body language,
these are very worrying caring people.
At last a little window snaps open.
A flushed face meets yours.
'Can I help you?' asks a voice.
'Yes, I'd like to speak to Mr — '
You give his personal name and title.
'Sorry! He's not in today.'
'May I...' The window closes again.
They are a people of few words.
You wait for a second chance.
Ten minutes later, the window opens.
'Can I help you?' It's the mechanical voice.
'May I speak to Mr —'s assistant?'
'Sorry! She's on sick leave.'
You hold on to the window
to prevent it from shutting.
'When will he be back, please?'
The face disappears and reappears.
'Not sure. Tomorrow. Next week.'
'I see,' you say, 'I'll come next year.'

The Alhambra Court of Lions

Tourists were on both pavilions
they were scrutinizing the arcades
they were squinting at the columns
they were gazing at the fountain.
Around this fountain, twelve stone lions
ten centuries old were spewing water.
In their eyes, as hard as flint
burnt all they had ever seen:
liaisons of this one and that
solemn promises and secret pacts
happy, loving couples joining hands
the smiles and laughter of friends
the despair and cries of treachery
all stored in their stone memory.
And now we were a part of the scene
New faces in the tourist stream.

The Skeleton from B.C.

If you could see yourself now
as others see you through a glass
not a semblance of what you were once —
how they gape at your hollow bones
that had buttressed your flesh and blood,
your throbbing life.

If you could see yourself now
as others see you through a glass,
well might you wonder that you,
a nobody, have become a celebrity.
From the millions tumbled in the dust,
you are preserved for posterity.

If you could see yourself now
as others see you through a glass,
well might you puzzle about things:
why you and not some other body
should be sitting in a showcase
staring at these peculiar beings.
Who knows who among those walking by,

two thousand years from now,
will be lying where you lie today
wondering like you about chance
and time and things that pass.

Much Ado About Something

People point to myriad shapes —
to hexagonals and octagonals,
to cubes, circles, diamonds — what have you.
They speak of the many patterns in nature,
of star-shaped and elongated creatures,
of the wonderful symmetry of you and me.
But who has consideration for the full stop,
that little dot, that obscure nothing
grammarians place at the close of a sentence
to indicate the end of a flow of thought?
A little gasp, a gulp of fresh air
a seal might take before diving again?
So often forgotten, so often neglected,
so often usurped by his more glamorous sister,
the shapely comma, touting her refinements
over paper and electronic media,
the full stop lives in monastic retirement.
But to me he is more than just 'Amen,'
more than 'That's it.' ' Basta.' ' C'est fini',
more than a pause for refreshing breath,
to me his shape signifies eternity.

He is a lot bigger than himself,
a lot bigger than meaning...
a microcosm of the black hole
into which crushed stars descend
when energy is spent and life is done.
He is the point at the end of a needle,
the pinprick from which life began,
a small promise of bigger things to come.

41

Murphy's Law

'If things can go wrong, they will go wrong' —
We have traced things to their source;
It's Murphy's Law, of course.
Why, otherwise, would the slice of toast
slip from your hands, butter side down?
Why does the quiet child start to cry
just when, tired out, you want to lie?
Why do you choose the shortest line
to find that it takes the longest time?
It's Murphy's Law, of course.
If you question the monk, he'll tell you
it's God's will. Even from bad, God derives good.
Things happen because God wills them.
If you question the guru, he'll tell you
it's destiny. Everything is in the plan.
Things happen because they must.
If you ask the gambler, he'll tell you
it's a question of good luck or bad luck.
Things happen because of chance.
If you question the philosopher, he'll tell you
it's all in the mind. There's nothing more.

Thinking about things makes them happen.
What if you try a more precise authority:
What does the mathematician have to say?
For him it's a matter of probability.
Things happen because of combinations.
And then we have Murphy's Law, of course:
'If things can go wrong, they will go wrong.'
We have traced things to their source —
We live in the worst of possible worlds.

The Dilemma

It was a case of hit and run,
the driver disappearing round the bend
of that lonely country road,
leaving me with the wriggling form.

And as I bent to examine the creature,
I became aware of the feline mother
crouched on the pavement, watching.
There were quick decisions to be made,
and so little time to make them.
Should I rush the kitten to the vet
leaving the mother alone to fret?
I could not take the mother without a fight
and there was no time for that.
There was a much easier way out.
I could put the kitten beside the mother
allowing chance decide one way or another.
A quick decision had to be made,
and there was no time to delay.

Bending down, I picked up my charge

and drove her away.
Long past the bend in the road,
I could sense those sad eyes —
watching — following at a distance.

Tipsy Mice

The guard at the bodega in Jerez
Fell asleep one sultry afternoon
On awakening he found his lunch gone
Nibbled by mice, perhaps a dozen strong
'Little devils,' he cried, 'this is a winery;
Would you like to booze on my sherry?'
He had a naughty idea at the time
Solera was a good tempting wine
He filled a glass with sweet solera
One that tasted of almond and honey
And placed it on the floor of the bodega
He leaned a ladder to its rim thinking it funny
He watched the mice pitter-patter to the top
They guzzled as if they would never stop.
Inebriated with the elixir they lost sleep
They romped and played hide and seek
They scampered around in euphoria
And missed orientation with the solera
Jumping helter-skelter here and there
As if they were diving in thin air
The winery was flattered

That mice were slurping the wine
It would be nice to use those mice
To advertise the wines of Jerez
The idea was quite daring and novel
How best to use them without trouble?
As for the rodents, the place is paradise
It mesmerises them with vapours
It energises them with spice
There is only one stipulation —
They must watch their reproduction
Or a shadowy sleuth comes to Eden
Pussyfooting all night long on light paws
Tom pounces on one and all with his jaws

The Road to Lakagígar

Our bus coughed its way
over the lava fields
to Lakagígar.
It coughed its way
over the domain for off-road vehicles,
not the domain for buses or bicycles.
Once on the road, there was no escape
over this moonscape.
It stumbled over rocks and boulders
It wobbled over grit and gravel
With the screeching of brakes
crossing rivers and pools of water
with breathless hydrophobia,
while all around the lava fields
stone figures, road sentinels, glared.
They must have thought we were mad.
Right across the road they stared,
as they watched our suicidal bus
panting for breath, courting death

The Icelandic Goðafoss

He looked up at the waterfall
How like a thundering monster
Crashing over stones and boulders
Frothing, heaving his shoulders
A monster full of anger
He looked down on the mound
Of gods at his feet
Idols carved from rock and stone
The temple stripped to the bone
One by one they went into the deep
And the people heard him cry:
'Begone all you gods of rock and moss
Become, O Waterfall, the Goðafoss
Swallow our idols one and all
For we have heard Another call'

The Blue Lagoon

As I approach the spa, I reel
Dizzy from the smell of sulphur
The miasma wraps round me, a cloak
Dark, dank and rank
Rocks, like hunched toads smoke
Surely I have been beguiled
Into Planet Hell
But wait a minute, they say
Walk out further — to the other side
What a wonderful Blue Lagoon
Spiraling stairways of steam fog the air
Eyes popping, I stand there and stare
It's a massive bubble bath, indigo blue
With vents of hazy hue
A thermal spa carved with ashen walls
Fringed in the distance with lava falls
Where people lie in various sprawls

As I step into the pool on a winter's day
38 degrees centigrade folds me like May
This lake is full of people young and old

They're here to shelter from the winter cold
Some smear their face, arms and hands
They come to swim, to float, to heal
In this Paradise
On this land called Ice

Kjölur Route

Elves of the Kjölur Route
Thank you for showing us the way
Hidden helpers clearing mist and soot
I feel, not hear what you say
'Ride softly, ride softly over the gravel
Ride softly, ride softly over the water
Ford it, ford it with ease
Here's a stone, a rock, a pebble
Here's another way — to disaster
Avoid it, avoid it, if you please'

Elves of the Kjölur way
I feel you, I feel your pull
As you steer us through the day
Between Langjökull and Hofsjökull
That pass between mountain kings
Broad sheets of glacial snow
With blinding peaks
And here are the Hveravellir Springs
Bubbling, bursting with flow
A show of nature's freaks

Invisible Elves of the Kjölur Way
Accept this stone I throw
Upon your mound today

Icebergs

Icebergs on the Jökulsárlón lakes
Dancers floating in lovely shapes
In your lagoon from the ice age
Draped in pink, white and blue
My camera eye has caught you
Your ice-blue and bright hue
Tinted by the cold arctic sun
In shining beauty next to none
My camera eye has caught your magic
If you melt it would be oh so tragic
If I could visit you when time has run
Will you still shine, diamonds in the sun?
A thousand, thousand years from now
Will you still be there to wow?
These eyes of mine will forever see you
Dancing phantoms in a sea of blue

The Bridge of Avignon

Only half of it still remains —
the bridge of Avignon.
A small crowd passing up and down
was trying to remember the song,
while a couple on the bridge
were arguing loudly in high pitch.
Like the Rhone monster enraged
she lashed out, the bridge her stage,
her eyes red as the setting sun,
spectators watching the fun.
'If you can't choose between us,
get the hell away from me.
Make up your bloody mind.
Don't come near me again.'
And the crowd went on listening:
'Sur le pont d'Avignon
L'on y danse
L'on y danse
Sur le pont d'Avignon
L'on y danse
Tout en rond.'

Traces of You

There are those fasteners on my duvet
and the wrap you knitted for a winter's day.
There's that needlepoint portrait
of the 'Mother and Child' on my bedroom wall.
There are trinkets in my jewel box
and perfumes on my dressing table.
On shelves, on sideboards, in every corner,
You've left memories of you.
Your bedroom slippers are where you left them.
Traces of you are everywhere —
On a warm summer's evening,
I see you in your rocking chair —

On the Slow Lane

The morning hangs around my neck, a stone
It bears me down with gravitating stealth
I sit in my car and watch the passing world alone —
Commuters rushing on their way to school or work
Cars, cars everywhere, tailbacks, bottlenecks
Only a snow drizzle and such mayhem
Most cars are inching their way with no brakes
Though some drivers still prefer the fast lane
The morning covers me with its heavy cloak
I start the day with long delays like other folk
The gas from engines is polluting on and on
The car behind toots; what have I done wrong?
Will my students fuss if I show up late for class?
A number of them may also miss the train or bus
With so much fretting there's no reason to talk
What's the use to focus only on the clock?

Nothing Much

Because the spring of the year
is wafting through my window,
memory opens wide its house:
your hand in mine
rough where a callus had formed,
our footsteps in the wet sand,
the wind in my hair.
Nothing much.
A knock on my door,
the drumming of my heart,
your voice, a glissando.
A bunch of daffodils,
elusive fragrances.
Nothing much.
And because the spring of the year
is wafting through my window
and memory is an open house,
I see you again as in a glass.

Obsession

I was caught
like a fish on an angler's hook.
When you looked at me, I fell headlong
into the gravity of your planet
And you said there was no other
But your talk was all of her:
her beauty, her elegance, her skills.
You were obsessed by her body parts.
Could you but see the passion on your face
when someone mentioned her name.
One night I watched you through a window:
saw you caress her body
saw the adrenaline on your face
as you gazed at her
saw you ride her up and down.
You did not really love me
You were driven by an obsession —
You were in love with that engine.

Thinking About Risks

Ask hang gliders or rock climbers
Ask bungee jumpers or water skiers
Ask acrobats, ask Evel Knievel
Sit them down, ask them how they do it
One thing and one thing alone is true
Thinking makes things detrimental
A vivid imagination makes risk suicidal
The pufferfish taster ensconced in candlelight
He sits forgetfully — fingering his delicacy
All his gustatory senses are on fire
The thinker in the gloom of his mind
Is watching him for dire reactions
He sees the white slivers on the plate
As death decorated and disguised
Has the restaurant the phone number
The phone number of a good doctor?
What traces of tetrodotoxin has his meal?
Is he soon going to hyperventilate —
His body to twitch with creepy insects —
His lips to tingle, his eyes to dilate —
Is he going to lie on a stretcher

In a coma and never recover?
One and one thing alone is true:
Imagination makes things detrimental
Where imagination rules, risk is suicidal.

The Exemplary Bee

There's something to be said for bees:
You never meet a workaholic bee
You never meet a bee doing overtime
It works in daylight when it can see
A bee slogs away in rain or shine
It has no time to stop and chat
A bee is too disciplined for that
There's something to be said for bees
After work to the hive they go
A bee has no time for an idle visit
No time for friends or foes
A bee will never stop to gossip
It has no time for owl or bat
A bee is too impartial for that
There's something to be said for bees
When work is done, they go home
To their queen, to quiet and peace
To social lives in their honeycomb
In their busy hub they sit and chat
Home is sweet, a bee knows that

The Neighbour's Cat

Dodo she was called, a misnomer
And she resented it too, I know
For she was a sleek sleuth
Coal black, with a white patch over one eye
She loved my garden where she could lie
Her mistress' garden was a slab of stone
Anaesthetized, polished, but not a home
In the sun it was a sterilized hospital floor
Dodo thought she was a terrible bore
My garden was her territorial zone
We were friends, Dodo and I from the start
'Dodo, Dodo' the neighbour would call
And Dodo pretended she wasn't there at all
We had a tacit understanding she and I
She could rely on me to be her ally
When her cleaning became an obsession
Dodo vanished, I guess from frustration
I looked for her everywhere in vain
Then she came back again
And sat there, a queen in my domain
'Why did you run away then?

I am happy to be your friend
I guess you couldn't take the smell
She thinks it's heaven; you think it's hell
Stay in my garden if here you feel well.'

Mosquito Power

Mosquitoes have become a mega power;
they are multiplying and quickly mutating,
acquiring super-skills, getting much bigger.
More than one hundred and fifty species strong,
they are preparing for the bloody onslaught
against puny man, around whom they throng
in great numbers. A Dracula by day and night,
the Anopheles female jabs her victim
often under cover, before taking flight.
Humans are slaves, providing her with shelter
in sewers, pools, water beds and dark places
where puny wrigglers and tumblers take cover.
Here fighter planes and guns are of no avail,
Neither will poison or pesticides suffice.
If something is not done, mosquitoes will prevail.

The Seagull's Flight

A flap of weak wings, an upward surge,
and the dizzy seagull was high in the sky.
He was a bereaved bird, singing a dirge.
Death was all along the beach,
moving like a bilious snake,
foaming, frothing, blood-curdling.
Black death with slimy tentacles —
asphyxiating.
All below him lay his brothers and sisters
with oily glazed eyes, their helpless wings
like molten lead, clinging to their lethal bed.
High above the black breakers, the curling vapours
the seagull soared, gasping for air, seeking his fill,
his nose, his compass still.

Snake Around the Neck

A lullabied snake can be a pet
baby around the charmer's neck.
Innocent as previously poisonous,
it wriggles in its warm bed.
The crowd knows it's potentially venomous.
They watch fascinated as the curvaceous
creature performs its belly dance
on the body of the man in a trance.
Sweet danger drugged to deceive,
snake around the neck.

The Spider's Web

I jackknifed a spider's web this morning.
A diaphanous thread was hanging
from the kitchen lamp, a gelatinous trap
dangling like gossamer from the ceiling.
Looking up, I saw through a little gap,
a spider peeping through her contoured map
at the collapsing stairway to her lair,
cheated of her breakfast by my mishap.
It was the perfect trap, as secret as air.
On my face it fell like a wisp of hair.
She must have given it careful thought,
the best place and time a fly to ensnare.
It was not remorse, it was not pity,
nor was it the spider's ingenuity
which prompted me to recompense her
with the very fly she would have caught.
It was sheer hatred of that pest
which routinely disturbs my rest.

The Answering Machine

I hear the disembodied voice, the beep-beep tone
I groan for I know there's nobody at home
Only that misnomer, that answering machine
Waiting silently for the message I bring
Recording automatically each paltry thing
My polished accent begins to shake
I fumble for language my tongue should make
I falter, I splutter, my words are jumbled
My mind is confused, my message is garbled
For I feel his steely eyes on me
And I know he's listening carefully
In the tomb of his impersonal mind
My words are enshrined
I cannot plead fear or dread
Or say I've made a mistake
In this austere court is my sentence passed
My judge, my prosecutor, unsurpassed.

The Push-Button

In the hurdy-gurdy world of high-tech machines
This modern world of gargantuan buildings
The paltry push-button controls everything
Invested with his royal title, 'Control Switch'
His index finger is at times on our breathing
In hospitals he can determine dying or living
At his random touch, doors open, doors close
Lifts go up and down, things get better or worse
At his imperious command, computers go down
Paralyzing the smooth running of the world
If you think of it, a simple touch of his icy hand
And life on this our planet can abruptly end

The Alarm's Rude Awakening

Why do you scream into my dream
Electronic thing with persistent ring
Can't you see I'm having fun
Brushing cobwebs from the sun
Dressing the sky with his rainbow tie
Riding the billowy clouds on high
Why do you scream into my dream
With your maniacal shrieking
With your hysterical beeping
Palpitating with nervous clicking
Can't you see I'm having a spree
As light as a bird and as free
Can't you see the butterflies and me
Under the flickering mulberry tree
Waltzing to the robin's magic flute
Singing to the starling's quivering lute
Answering to the brown owl's toot
Can't you hear the plaintive cricket
In the lush yellow-green thicket
Complaining to the droning bee
Humming his tune in minor key

Can't you hear the woodpecker's beak
Tap-tapping on the stone-hard teak
Unceremonious voice of noise
Why do you scream into my dream?
Rude Awakener with your noisy bell
Sounding the loud-clanging knell
On my surreal world of lovely dreams
Rushing me back to practical things

City Noises at Night

The noises of the city are alive at night:
the screeching brakes, the slamming doors
loud laughter and muffled moans
the grating saw with vice-like teeth
the pneumatic drill crunching stone
raised voices above the din.
The sounds of the city disturb the night:
the drunken man with unseeing eyes
feeling his way, cursing the darkness.
Homeless wanderers, stoned, cold
sleep walkers estranged from the fold
arguing loudly with an alien world.
The noises of the city slaughter the night:
a fire-eating, fire-breathing beast
with red silhouette, lapping the miles
ringing its urgent alarm
a panther, veteran night hunter
with flashing eyes, stalking the enemy
and toot-tooting at its prey
a howling hyena mourning the dead
with wailing sirens, hysterical.

The city, a towering monster
boxed within its cacophonic walls
stamps on and tramples the night.

Mirror Images

In the broken glass on the floor,
I see myself all in fragments:
an eye, half of an arm, a toe,
nothing whole, everything in segments.
I can live with disparate elements;
distorted images are just accidental.
Fragmented pieces are no impediments.
More disturbing to nature would be
carbon copies of us all, 'look-alikes'
Not fragments in a glass but quintuplets
of the same person, real people clones.
How should I recognise me if I moved in multiples?
Goodbye it would be to all that's unique and original.
Goodbye it would be to all that's natural and normal.

Night Light (motion sensor)

Dazzling Electric Eye
Focusing on and off
In your niche aloft
Tell me
What do you see from high?
What do you reflect?
What do you detect?
I tell you —
It's only the garden gnome
Tramping the ground
It's only the garden gnome
Making his round —
With his patchwork quilt of leaves
He's blanketing the birds and the bees
He's closing the windows of the flowers
From the cold night showers
He's bolting all the doors of the mole holes
And covering the spider with his robe folds
Powerful Scrutinizing Beams
With halogenous gleams
Tell me —

What do you feel out there?
I tell you —
It's only the cold night air
And the garden gnome guarding the house
Of the little field mouse
From that wily thief
Cat on padded feet
Searching for his meat
Potent Private Eye
Tell me —
What do you think you see?
I tell you —
It's only the garden gnome
Rocking the colic sparrow
In the wheelbarrow
It's only the garden gnome
Under the apple tree
The garden gnome — walking free.

Castle Fantasy

Day by day visitors streamed into the old museum
studying the exhibits — antediluvian.
And one by one they passed the centrepiece,
a model castle with Gothic portcullis.
They stopped and looked with idle, casual glance,
seeing the tower steepling high into the sky,
the courtyard, the drawbridge, the murky moat.
And some, a privileged some, saw the little boat.
But there came a small boy whose lingering gaze
took in the enchanted castle, ablaze
with bewitching lights; he saw the knight,
who, winking, whisked him away
to the great wall-walk, the allure
into lovely, elaborate chambers
adorned with tapestries and draperies,
where lords and ladies sauntered into the hall,
preparing for the glittering, royal ball.
And the small boy talked and walked
with that charming knight of yore
who took him to the minstrels' gallery
where the troubadours and jesters make merry,

and where he split his sides laughing
at the court jester's red stocking.
Then he went into the scullery and buttery
and finally into the emblazoned armoury.
And as he looked all spellbound,
the knight spoke, and at the sound,
the room was suddenly transformed
into a fantastic playground
with knights jousting and fencing,
their shields and lances gleaming.
As sword clashed with sword, and shield with shield,
Boy and knight boldly joined the field.

The Loreley

The ship is drifting along the river Rhine
with silver painted prow and festive flags.
The proud captain has no real use for maps,
for he has plied the river many a time.
All along the Rhine, the weather is fine,
spirits high, wine flowing as water from taps,
when the crew hear a bewitching song from the crags.
It is the temptress, Loreley, calling them to dine.
They see her lovely form upon the rock;
they hear the strains of her sensuous voice
beckoning to them in seductive tones.
Drunk with the fruit of the vine, they cannot stop
their palpitating hearts. There is a loud noise,
a crack, and the ship is wrecked upon the stones.

The Museum Artifact

I stand in awe before the broken pots and pans
Pieced — mended by dedicated hands
As the light dances upon the burnished urn
The eyes of the mighty Zeus glow and burn
And then my mind begins to whirl and swirl
And like someone blind, I plunge helplessly
Backward — in time
Slowly at first, then faster and faster
An unstoppable juggernaut in reverse gear
Past genteel lords and ladies bedecked in finery
Past unassailable castles with drawbridge moats
Past knights in brilliant armour
Looking on in speechless wonder —
Further, further, a tremendous backward lurch
Past that old edifice, the Roman church
Where puff-cheeked cherubs playing the horn
Sing the song of an awakening dawn
Past those stately sentinel stones
Jealous guardians of buried bones
Stones inscribed with mysterious runes
Defying the transience of living things

Down, down the dusty time tunnels
Past the strong Roman fortresses
Straight roads, intricate walls, buttresses
And the hanging vineyard with ripening grape
Bequeathing Europe its cultural shape
And Time stands still at last in ancient Greece
As I gaze longingly in surprised wonder
At the beauty, the knowledge, the power
The unconquerable spirit of Man —
Dashing the cup of hemlock from Socrates
I yearn for the wisdom — for which I've come
But wisdom echoes through the halls of time
And still I stand before that magic urn
And still the eyes of Zeus glow and burn

The Stifled Poem

In the black hole of my mind,
indistinguishable somethings,
like atoms securely locked,
a hard core of unborn nothings
are strangulating, striving to find
a sudden burst of release.
In a diffusion of white light,
a vague little shape is set free.
I feel it all around my head;
I cannot hear, I cannot see,
give it body, or make it bright.
Is it doomed to death or disease?
Stillborn child of my restless brain,
I would that I could give you life,
warm you, adorn you, make you grow,
send you there where strife is rife
as a torch-bearer, a light for life.
But here I lie, languishing,
overcome by creative anguish.
Striving for the birth of an idea
that would take shape and colour.

The Streets of Oxford

I have seen the homeless on the streets of Oxford,
happy people hunched in secluded corners,
bundled like mummies for the night.
Young and old, they lie in the cold,
spending time's vacuum in company or alone,
talking and laughing but never crying.
Under a grey nimbus cloud, I saw you crying,
twisted in a knot on a street in Oxford.
Spire-gazing, I stumbled into you there alone,
legs outstretched between two little corners.
Confused, I turned from you in the cold,
Turned to my little world, my comfort zone.
Your ravaged face still haunts my night.
I see you, folded in wrinkles, crying.
I see me tripping along, callous and cold,
with my head aloft in the clouds of Oxford.
How can I help lodgers in rutted corners,
not knowing what it feels to be all alone?
Was there a time when you were not alone?
Was that the thing on your mind that night?
or were your thoughts on cosy domestic corners?

Alas! I shall never know why you were crying
when I was walking that street in Oxford
with my head high and my heart cold.
I cannot link lofty spires with boxed corners
where waif-like women are blue with cold.
If those timeless stones could speak out,
would it not be for those sitting alone,
in corners where great minds mingle
up and down the streets of Oxford?

72

The Blue Grotto of Capri

Are there mermaids in the Blue Grotto?
Mermaids with azure faces and golden tails
Sitting in silver ships with painted sails
Mermaids with flashing mirrors in their hands
Playing with jets of light from outside lands?
Are there nymphs in the cobalt waters?
Singing softly from dawn to noon
Dancing freely round the moon
Nymphs with ruby lips and pearly eyes
Shimmering and glimmering under the skies?
Are there wicked witches in the Blue Grotto?
Witches and elves in close conspiracy
Beguiling the idle wanderer on his way
With fantastic watercolour display
Conjuring with wily stratagems
A world of fantastic diadems?
Are their unknown gods in the turquoise waters?
Gods with shining sons and daughters
Displaying the splendour of their super might
In yellow, blue-green, purple, rainbow light?
These secrets I will never know

I have only seen their access door
An open mouth, frothing and foaming
With loud sounds of their breathing
But the message is loud and clear
'I tell thee, do not enter here.'

Spirit of the Catacombs

I stood in the crowd all alone,
eyes wandering in bewildered gaze
down the tumbling maze upon maze.
And then I came face to face
with him.
Mouldy with age, lean and tall,
bones knocking against the wall,
he stretched forth one wizened hand,
and I felt the hollow voice say,
his cadaverous voice holding mine
with magnetic sway:
'Get thee from hence! Away!'
Petrified, I turned to flee, but stood transfixed
as the eyes, like torches in the darkness
compelled me into that everlasting maze.
'Fiend or Angel, turn your eyes away;
tell me your name I boldly pray.'
But nought could I hear, only the echoes,
nought could I see, only the shadows,
and the gaunt figure with the luminescent orbs.
I could not see, but I could feel

his awful presence at my heel.
And then I heard them call
from every quarter of that subterranean hall.
Voices, sepulchral voices loudly yelling:
'Who is this that dares disturb our dwelling?'
Shapes loomed large upon the crypts,
shapes resurrecting from the pits.
Wild, uncanny, shapeless shapes
draped only in parchment threads.
Fear, cold fear, clutched at my heart,
lending wings to my numbed feet.
And I ran like one possessed
through the meandering maze,
up and down and round and round
the dim passageways and alleyways,
the merry-go-round winding and twisting,
never-ending, turning ever more and more.
At every turn, at every corner,
there he stood, that dreaded taunter
looming large as life, but still as death.
And ever at my back, the mocking leer,
echoing in the hollows, loud and clear,
'Who is it? Who is it a-coming here,
disturbing this our sacred sphere?'
And still pursued, I ran all trembling
toward the one dim light filtering
from a distant crypt.
Surely it must be the crypt of St Cecilia.
A thrill of joy ran down my spine;
victory, at last, was mine.

Down St Cecilia's aisle
was escape, the exit door
leading to the open moor.
Ignoring the pursuing feet,
the gasping breath, the suffocating heat,
I dashed through that elusive door,
and found myself upon the floor
OUTSIDE — in the bright awakening light.

Through the Channel Tunnel

When they were tunnelling through the rock
to hundreds of meters below the sea,
when giant machines were busy chewing
with claw-like teeth through impervious maul,
when concrete enough for Egyptian pyramids
was hauled in for the walls of the Channel Tunnel,
people stood by, watching the undertaking
with awe, with scepticism and with dread.
What if the roof comes cascading
and the tunnel is squashed flat
collapsing on top of a racing train?
What if pressure creates cracks and gaps
and the water suddenly rushes in
flooding everything in an instant?
What if there is a violent collision,
or a fire, or an earthquake?
Now that tunnel has become for me
much like any other railway tunnel.
The train speeds from Brussels to the tunnel;
twenty minutes it runs the mechanical tube,
and then it noses out into England.

From my bright and ventilated cocoon,
the darkness outside reveals nothing.
There are no stalactites or stalagmites,
there are no scenic rococo formations
caused by dissolving droplets of water.
Beyond the darkness are tons of concrete —
to the right, to the left, over my head —
Beyond the concrete are mountains of rock,
Beyond that is the teeming marine life.
The daylight at the end of the tunnel
reveals to me a vast green paradise,
and it always comes as a surprise
to realise that I am out of the funnel.

The Ice Cream Man

Two o'clock and Charlotte would shout:
'Here comes the ice cream man,'
and how fast all the children ran
We'd hear the ting-a-ling-a-ling of the bicycle bell;
With his umbrella his shield, he was ready to sell
It became an afternoon ritual
The children gathering to see
Charlotte, Jason, Ming Lee and me —
We were the lucky ones with money
Each of us bent on the coveted popsicle
Beside the ice cream box was a gadget
A wheel with numbers from one to ten
You pay for a lolly, and turn the 'tikam' wheel
Round and round it spun before it would stop
On your lucky number; one you always got.
Jason was the luckiest of us all
He often got two for the price of one
Snatching his sticks, he would run
All we wanted were two little licks
From those chocolatey sticks
I was the unluckiest of the four

One was all that I could score
But one time I dropped my coin
I turned the wheel; it fell on ten
It was like a magic touch
I was able to share so much
Then suddenly, the ice cream man was not there
We waited and waited for him in the square
And Charlotte cried: 'Here comes the ice cream man — '
And we all dropped everything and ran
It was a wish, for she had not heard his bell
Decades have passed, but I still hear
Charlotte's voice loud and clear:
'Here comes the ice cream man.'
And still I see Jason near the stand
And sometimes I think I hear the bell.

A Mechanical World?

The professor and the computer were talking
in the wee hours of the morning.
Said the computer in a humble tone:
'Give me a chance to guard your home
to do your chores and close your doors
to mind the baby and clean your floors
to walk your dog and run your errands:
you don't have to live at sixes and sevens.
Just give me a chance
your life to enhance.'
Said the professor appraisingly,
'I accept you're amazingly
quick, efficient and busy.'
Said the computer, 'That's easy.
Just give me a chance
my mind to advance
to run your life with precision
to rule your world with decision.
My brain is bigger, my memory better,
You'll admit I'm cleverer.'
Said the professor in fury

'How dare you! That's vainglory.
Just a tool you'll always be
I'll not change you for a fee.'
'Admit,' droned the voice,
not without some noise:
'Man is vanquished by death and disease
while we multiply and increase.'
Said the professor, 'A virus can destroy you:
I tell you there are more than a few.'
Said the computer imperiously,
'Your Darwin had a theory:
the fittest shall survive
in this world of strife.
You're superior to the ape,
a law it cannot escape,
and I'm superior to man;
it's all in the plan.'
The professor was thinking
his head sorely aching:
It wasn't too late
to mend a mistake.
The world run by a machine —
Preposterous! The error supreme.

Morse Code

Of late if you write letters, you're a bore
And to many people it's an awful chore
Text messaging on smart phones is the rave
It's quick and fast and you can stop and save
Some people laugh if you write a postcard
They consider you a real old diehard
Letters and cards belong to the past
But that old Morse Code, it lasts and lasts
Easy and simple to use, it's not hard or coarse
It stands defiant and clear, without bias
Used during the war, it's in fact timeless
In Morse you don't have to utter an 'e'
It's just a tap, a flash you hear or see
The Morse of dots and dashes is clear
We know what 'dit dit dit dah dah dah dit dit dit' can mean
In the sand it reads: ... - - - ... and we rush to the scene

Stranger

The six-eyed creature came plummeting down
the opposite way around
through the dim stairways of space
all in a daze.
His space suit was ripped
his flying boots flipped
as on a cloud he landed
curious, utterly bewildered.
Peering through the white skies
with his telescopic eyes
he saw the blue planet at last
with people walking fast.
'It's plain to see,' sighed he,
'the creatures of earth aren't like me.
Their eyes are not in position
they have limited vision.
Their side eyes are cute
shrivelled flaps, quite mute.
Their rear eyes are very furry
These people are in such a hurry.'
The six-eyed creature stared in surprise

such hurry must only end in demise.
'They come in different colours and shapes
and they wear such flimsy drapes.
Some are short, and some are lean
strange mutation of a gene.'
His focused vision scanned frame and face
then delving, went straight to the base.
'Why,' said he 'their powers aren't good
they can't recycle their food.
A red river runs like a throbbing main
from the heart to the brain.
Their houses are big and tall
Looks like they could fall.
Some can run on all fours
these are rows and rows
emitting vapour and smoke
it could make you choke.
The creatures of earth aren't like me
away from this planet I'll flee.'
'Thank you,' he whispered, 'for the code you sent
you'll never know I came and went.'

The Workaholic

The veiled moon sheds her wan and shadowy light
on the pale face of the man working the night.
Compressed across the tightrope of time,
his body, responding to mounting pressure,
like the strings of a Stradivarius
stretch and strain to their fullest measure.
But tautly tuned strings across a bow
break under a rushing tempo.
His body, a ticking device fully wired,
awaits that fatal moment when it is fired,
but anaesthetized against every human pain,
he cannot hear warning signals from his brain.

The Intercity Express Train

Like a tapering millipede with electric feet,
sleek, long-distance runner, the intercity train —
with hundred lighted windows and gushing heartbeat
thumping from that powerful engine, the super-brain —
is whooshing into tunnels, climbing or descending,
whizzing round corners with dignified precision,
silvery body glittering, shining eyes exploring
till they come to rest on the distant horizon.
I sit ensconced in layers of warmth — half dreaming,
watching present time merge into hazy past.
Houses, mountains, hills, trees, everything now emerging
in a twinkling, are just memories stirred by the dust.
The future once expressed is again the past;
expectation is best, nothing in time can last.

Yesterday's Leaves

Here we sit on the top of the mountain
last year's leaves at our feet,
the city below us, a sleeping dwarf.
Your cheeks are as red as raspberries.
I wonder what we'll both do
when our legs start to drag,
lugging our bodies like wet logs,
when three hundred steps up Salisbury cathedral
become pictures in a video camera.
What will I do when the live coals of your eyes
smoulder to ashes?
What will you do when I don't know
today from tomorrow or yesterday?
The answer is in the susurrus
of dead leaves at our feet.

The Telescope

A long tube mounted on a tripod
Man's truly marvellous discovery
Dream window.
A slight turn of the wheel
And millions of light years reel
Away into nothingness.
Magic eyepiece
Revealing but a small vision of Immensity.
A microcosm
Of the vast Tremendousness of space.
Shimmering Venus
Resplendent, magnificent
Riding the heavens:
A moon scythe
Caught on a wonder glass
Beautiful, gaseous, poisoned crystal ball.
Mighty Jupiter with revolving moons
Trembling between a tripod
Spinning round and round
Like a cosmic mobile
Fragile.

Wafted as if by a gentle whiff
An ethereal breeze.
Optical illusion
Of that colossal giant unvisited by time
Powerful assailant
Pushing, pulling, exerting, swerving
With strange gravitational wings
The course of passing things.
And our Milky Way, a mere nothing
In that vast Infinity
Never ending galaxies stretching, stretching
More and yet more, further and further
Receding, escaping, eluding Time and Space
Region upon region of unplumbed sky
Shining, shimmering, shattering stars
Glittering canopy of diamonds.
Collisions, explosions
Creating glorious supernovae
Soundless cacophony.
Dying stars extinguishing fire
Plunging into black holes
Sucking, slurping, surrendering
To unfathomable and unfathomed
New worlds.

The Covid-19 Pandemic

How dare you wear a crown, Covid
How dare you think you're a hit
What are you now? Just another cipher
Covid-19 by any other name, still a viper
You skipped rank, you spiky little virus
But Man is brave and will fight this crisis
Up in arms we come, young and old
Those you attack are brave and bold
They'll fight you with their last breath
Some succumb but many live in health
Hope is our banner, Covid, you shall die
We'll never give up; return to your sty
We want you gone from hospitals and home
Gone, gone with no place on earth to roam
If you persist you will be wiped out soon
Our experts are preparing your doom
A vaccine will put an end to your reign
The shining crown will be ours in the end

The Masked Year

Masked two thousand and twenty where were you going
With your face so sad and your voice so still?
Regardless, the care-less Danube kept on flowing
Where were the voices of tourists so loud and shrill?
Where were the small skiffs that glided the water?
Where were the pleasure cruisers, where the sound?
Where the laughter, where the clicking of the camera?
Your silence was loud, I heard it bound and rebound
There were no voices of children in the playground
Masked two thousand and twenty, I missed your voice
The voice of the canal water, the voice of noise
As I sat by the window, how I missed your joys
The streets were sorry looking, the people scared
Our cities were closed, we had become like foes
We walked past each other, and people glared
The joy, the laughter, the hellos were missed most
What had happened to the hurry of the big city?
Where were the airplanes flying over the skies?
Where was our past life so busy and whizzy?
Now we were scared to look another in the eyes
Day, night, I heard the complaining voice of sirens

The ambulance wailing on distant horizons
Masked 2020 you were lost in distant environs.
But hurrah! you're back again in summery July
And I hear the voices of children on the green
As people meet and greet and refuse to die
May our summer holiday be happy and clean
As you smile once more with your head held high
I guess you will not be the year that said goodbye

The Whistling Poet

(For Howard Nemerov)

The path from class to Olin Library
Is strewn with leaves from ginkgo trees
Stately boughs where birds find sanctuary
They now are bare as beaches washed by seas —
The green of yesterday so quickly turned
To sunset hues, to rust and ruddy brown
The leaves of such trees are burned
By time, but fall does not cast them down
I walk along with thoughts of Nature's way
when suddenly I hear a happy whistling tune
It hangs upon the air, a lingering roundelay
I turn and wave, he's gazing out his room
Poet Laureate, your happy songs I hear
Your poems laugh and cry, soothe and cheer
You're gone but your poetry lives on
Immortal poet whose face was a song

The Full Stop

How important is the tiny full stop
To forget it is to ramble on until you drop
It is a microcosm of the black hole
Into which crushed stars descend
When energy is spent and life is done
It is the point at the end of a needle
The pinprick from which life sprung.

Mavis Donner received her Ph.D. in English from Washington University in St. Louis, Missouri, USA. She has been an English teacher and lecturer at several schools and universities around the world and at Webster University in Leiden, The Netherlands, where she lectured for 22 years, teaching English composition, literature and creative writing. The Writers' Circle she set up there for writers met regularly to discuss and share their talents. She is a published writer of poetry and short story anthologies, and her short story 'Mata Hari' was broadcast by the BBC World Service. She lives in Vienna, Austria.